FAMOUS PEOP

FA

D0352133

Biographies of famous people to
support the curriculum.

Henry VIII

by Harriet Castor

Illustrations by Peter Kent

W

FRANKLIN WATTS

LONDON•SYDNEY

First Published in 1999
by Franklin Watts
This edition 2001

Franklin Watts
96 Leonard Street
London EC2A 4XD

Franklin Watts Australia
56 O'Riordan Street
Alexandria, Sydney
NSW 2015

ISBN 0 7496 4320 X

A CIP catalogue record for this book is
available from the British Library

Dewey Decimal Classification
Number:942.05

10 9 8 7 6 5 4 3

Series Editor: Sarah Ridley
Consultant: Dr Anne Millard

Printed in Hong Kong

Henry VIII

In 1501 there was a royal wedding in London. The King and Queen's eldest son, Prince Arthur, married a Spanish princess called Catherine of Aragon. Arthur's younger brother, Henry, led Catherine up the aisle.

Henry had grown up thinking he was going to be an important nobleman, or perhaps a powerful priest.

But five months after the wedding, Prince Arthur fell ill and died. Now Henry was the heir to the throne. His father made sure he was kept safe.

Then, when Henry was seventeen, his father died too. Henry became King Henry VIII.

One of the first things Henry did as king was to marry Catherine, the Spanish princess. Royal marriages were a good way of making an alliance, or friendship, between countries. Spain was an important and powerful country. Besides, Henry and Catherine liked each other.

Because Catherine was the widow of Henry's brother, Henry had to ask the Pope for special permission to marry her.
The Pope said yes.

Henry was everyone's idea of what a king should be. He was tall, handsome and sporty. He was good at languages and music. He loved hunting, dancing, feasting, and wearing fine clothes.

Government meetings bored Henry, and he hated writing letters. But he made sure his ministers told him everything that happened. They left all the most important decisions to him.

What is it, man? I'm going hunting.

Could you just sign this, Your Grace?

Henry's chief minister was a priest called Cardinal Wolsey. Unlike most people at Court, Wolsey hadn't been born into an important family.

Wolsey was clever and worked hard, and Henry trusted him. Many of the nobles were jealous of Wolsey's power. They especially hated him because he came from an ordinary family.

Wolsey's palace is magnificent.

Henry believed great kings should be great warriors, so he wanted to go to war. He decided to attack France, one of England's oldest enemies.

Henry sailed to France with his army. He didn't take part in the fighting himself, but his soldiers won a battle. Henry came home triumphant.

Soon the old French king died. The new king, François I, was young and athletic. Henry was curious to meet him, so Wolsey arranged it.

The meeting took place on the border between Calais – a town England owned then – and the rest of France. Everywhere was decorated with gold cloth, so people called the place 'The Field of the Cloth-of-Gold'.

Henry and Catherine had been married for nearly twenty years. They had had several children, but only one had survived: a daughter, Mary.

A woman can't rule! It would be a disaster!

Henry wanted a son. He thought that only men were good at ruling countries.

Then Henry fell in love with one of Catherine's maids of honour, Anne Boleyn. She was young, witty and clever. He wanted to marry her.

I'm sure Anne could give me a son.

Henry had begun to think that God was cross with him for marrying Catherine, his brother's widow. He wanted the new Pope to say that, in God's eyes, they had never truly been married.

The trouble was, Catherine's nephew Charles was the **King of Spain**. He was very powerful. The Pope knew if he agreed to do what Henry wanted, **Charles** would be angry.

The Pope made promises to both Charles and Henry. But he didn't keep them. Eventually, he sent a cardinal (an important priest) to England to judge the case for divorce. The cardinal he chose was old and ill.

When the case began, Catherine knelt at Henry's feet. She said she was his true wife. Then she left the courtroom and refused to come back.

Still there was no decision. Henry was angry. He blamed Wolsey and sent him to prison. But Wolsey fell ill and died on the way.

Then Anne Boleyn became pregnant. Henry had to marry her quickly so that the baby could be next in line to the throne.

So Henry's ministers persuaded Parliament to pass a law saying that *Henry* was head of the Church in England, and he could judge the divorce case himself. Henry divorced Catherine.

It's not up to the Pope. I'm divorced and that's that.

At this time, people all over Europe were arguing about the right way to worship God. One group, Catholics, supported the Pope. Another group, later called Protestants, were against the Pope. Many people were put to death.

Henry didn't like either side. He was against the Pope, but he was also against many things the Protestants believed in.

Henry wanted his subjects to believe only what he told them.

Henry ordered that every monastery and nunnery should be shut down. His new chief minister, Thomas Cromwell, organised it for him.

Henry said it was because the monks and nuns weren't living a holy life. They were greedy and lazy. This was true in some cases but not all. Many of the monasteries had lots of money and land, which Henry wanted.

Meanwhile, Anne had her baby. It was a girl, called Elizabeth. Henry was disappointed and cancelled his planned celebrations. He didn't know that Elizabeth would one day be a great ruler.

Still no son! God must think this marriage is wrong, too.

Anne got pregnant twice more, but lost the babies. Henry was angry. He had already fallen in love with someone else: one of Anne's ladies-in-waiting, called Jane Seymour.

Anne was put in prison. She was accused of plotting to murder Henry and of having affairs with several men. None of it was true, but Anne and the men had their heads chopped off. Straight afterwards, Henry married Jane.

The next year Jane had a baby boy, Edward. But Jane died a few days later. Henry was very sad.

Because royal marriages were a useful way of making friendships between countries, Thomas Cromwell started looking for a new wife for Henry right away.

Whenever a possible wife was suggested, Henry wanted to know what she looked like.
So the famous painter, Hans Holbein, was sent to paint her.

One of the people Holbein painted was the daughter of a German duke – Anne of Cleves.

Henry agreed to marry Anne. When she landed in England, he was so impatient to meet her that he arrived early, in disguise.

But Henry didn't like what he saw. He was angry with Cromwell for arranging the marriage.

Many of the nobles were glad. They were jealous of Cromwell's power and hated him because, like Wolsey, he came from an ordinary family.

Henry had already noticed a new young woman at Court. Her name was Katherine Howard. The Howards were powerful nobles who hated Cromwell. They began plotting against him.

Cromwell was put in the Tower of London. As Henry's minister, he had invented a new way for important prisoners to be executed without trial. It was used for the first time – on him.

Cromwell worked hard for Henry. Henry will regret this ...

Since Henry was Head of the Church, it was easy for him to divorce Anne of Cleves. Anne didn't argue. Henry gave her plenty of money to live on.

Now Henry was free to marry his sweetheart, Katherine Howard. She was five years younger than Mary, Henry's daughter. She was cheerful and lively, but foolish, too.

Before her marriage, Katherine had had several secret lovers.

She had fallen in love with an ambitious but charming courtier called Thomas Culpeper. Soon she started seeing him again.

Like every powerful family, the Howards had enemies. Some of them found out about Katherine's affair and told Henry. Henry was grief-stricken and furious. He had Katherine and her lover executed.

As his sixth wife Henry chose a young widow called Catherine Parr. She was intelligent, and kind to his children. She was also good at nursing Henry.

Even Catherine had enemies at Court. There was a plot against her, but she found out just in time. She rushed to Henry, and explained that her enemies had told him lies.

At last, aged fifty-five, Henry died. He was buried, as he'd ordered, next to Jane Seymour at Windsor Castle. Their son – the boy Henry had longed for – became King Edward VI.

More about Henry VIII

Rhyme to remember
There is a rhyme that makes it easy to remember what happened to each of Henry's six wives:

Divorced, beheaded, died,
Divorced, beheaded, survived.

Can you name them all (without looking back through the book?)

H&A, H&K, H&C, H&J
In Henry's time, royal buildings were often decorated with the initials of the king and queen. But Henry had so many queens that wood-carvers and window-makers were always having to change the initials. Sometimes the old initials survived. Today, if you go to

St James's Palace in London, for example, you can still see the initials of Henry and Anne Boleyn, who was only the second of his six wives.

Henry Tudor

Henry's family name was Tudor. His father, Henry VII, had been the first Tudor king. Henry VIII hoped that the Tudor family would reign for a long time. In fact, they lasted only as long as his children. All three became monarchs – as King Edward VI, Queen Mary I and Queen Elizabeth I. None of them had children of their own, so the Tudor line came to an end.

Some important dates in Henry VIII's lifetime

1491 Henry is born in Greenwich, near London, the third child of King Henry VII and his wife, Elizabeth of York.

1502 Arthur, Prince of Wales – Henry's older brother – dies.

1509 Henry VII dies and Henry becomes King Henry VIII.

1509 Henry marries his brother's widow, Catherine of Aragon.

1516 Henry and Catherine's daughter, Princess Mary, is born.

1520 Henry meets the young French king, Francois I, at the Field of the Cloth-of-Gold.

1533 Henry declares that the Pope has no special authority in England; *he* is head of the Church.

1533 Queen Anne Boleyn gives birth to a girl, Princess Elizabeth.

1537 Queen Jane Seymour gives birth to a boy, Prince Edward. Jane dies twelve days later.

1540 Henry marries Anne of Cleves. He divorces her soon afterwards.

1540 Henry marries Katherine Howard.

1543 Henry marries Catherine Parr.

1547 Henry dies, aged fifty-five. He is buried in St George's Chapel, Windsor Castle.